UN!CORNS

ASHLEY GISH

MYTHICAL
X
CREATURES

NORTH
AMERICA

EUROPE

ASIA

AFRICA

SOUTH
AMERICA

AUSTRALIA

CREATIVE EDUCATION · CREATIVE PAPERBACKS

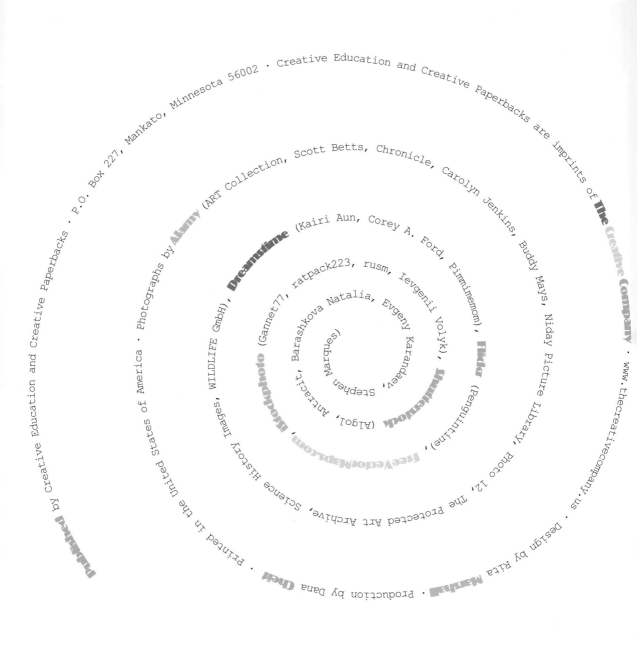

Published by Creative Education and Creative Paperbacks • P.O. Box 227, Mankato, Minnesota 56002 • Creative Education and Creative Paperbacks are imprints of The Creative Company • www.thecreativecompany.us • Design by Rita Marshall • Production by Dana Cheit • Printed in the United States of America • Photographs by Alamy (ART Collection, Scott Betts, Chronicle, Carolyn Jenkins, Buddy Mays, Niday Picture Library, Photo 12, The Protected Art Archive, Science History Images, WILDLIFE GmbH), Dreamstime (Kairi Aun, Corey A. Ford, Pimmimemom), freevectormaps.com (Gannet77, ratpack223, rusm, Ievgenii Volyk), iStock (Penguiritine), Shutterstock (Algol, Antracit, Barashkova Natalia, Evgeny Karandaev, Stephen Marques)

Library of Congress Cataloging-in-Publication Data • Names: Gish, Ashley, author. • Title: Unicorns / Ashley Gish. • Series: X-books: mythical creatures. • Includes index. • Summary: A countdown of five of the most intriguing unicorn encounters provides thrills as readers learn about the legendary characteristics of these mythical creatures. • Identifiers: LCCN: 2018038396 / ISBN 978-1-64026-198-3 (hardcover) / ISBN 978-1-62832-761-8 (pbk) / ISBN 978-1-64000-316-3 (eBook) • Subjects: LCSH: Unicorns—Juvenile literature. Classification: LCC GR830.U6 G57 2019 / DDC 398.24/54—dc23 • CCSS: RI.3.1-8; RI.4.1-5, 7; RI.5.1-3, 8; RI.6.1-2, 4, 7; RH.6-8.3-8
First Edition HC 9 8 7 6 5 4 3 2 1 • First Edition PBK 9 8 7 6 5 4 3 2 1

UN!CORNS

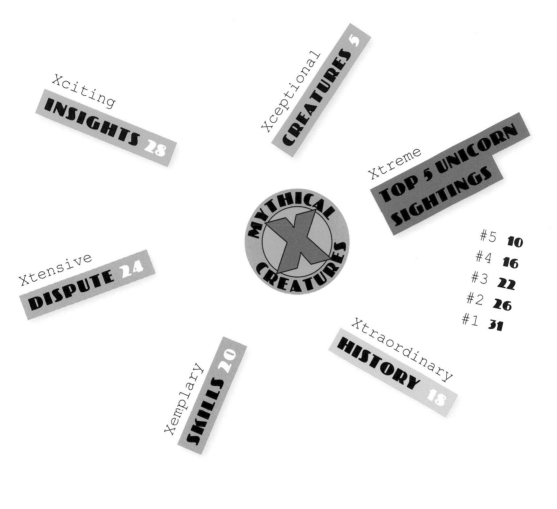

XCEPTIONAL CREATURES

A unicorn is a mythical animal. A single horn grows on its forehead. **Legends** describe unicorns as white horses. They have been featured in stories for thousands of years.

Unicorn Basics

Thousands of years ago, a Greek traveler wrote about **exotic**, mysterious places. He claimed to have seen unicorns. Their bodies were white, and their heads were red. He compared them to donkeys. But their hooves were cloven. This means each hoof was split into two parts. Cows, goats, and deer have cloven hooves. The animal he saw was probably an Arabian oryx. It is a type of antelope. It has straight, ringed horns. These can be more than two feet (0.6 m) long.

"UNICORN" SIGHTINGS

Throughout history, many unique animals have been mistaken for unicorns.

OKAPIS

The horse-sized okapi is found in African rainforests. Male okapis have a pair of horns.

EUROPE

AFRICA

ARABIAN ORYX

Pale in color with cloven hooves and long horns, the oryx is found on the Arabian Peninsula.

ASIA

SAOLAS

Rarely seen, these two-horned animals live in Vietnam near Laos.

RHINOCEROSES

Different rhinos can be found in Africa and Asia. They sport one or two horns.

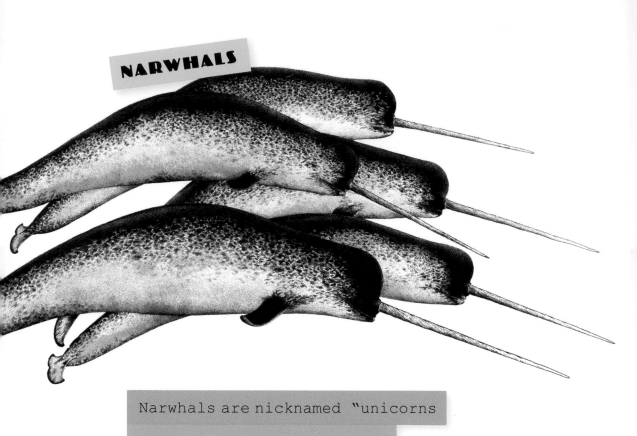

NARWHALS

Narwhals are nicknamed "unicorns of the sea." Their tusks can be nearly 10 feet (3 m) long.

Over time, unicorns were described as looking like horned horses. They kept their cloven hooves. They are usually white. But they can be any color, even silver or pink.

Unicorn horns are called alicorns. They are magical. It was once thought that, when ground into a powder, alicorn could cure illnesses and counteract poisons. Alicorn powder was used in medicine as recently as 1741. But what were people really using? Some "alicorns" were probably the spiraling tusks of narwhals. Others may have been rhinoceros horns.

Unicorns can sense lies and evil thoughts.

LIE X DETECTORS

UNICORN BASICS FACT

The name "unicorn" is taken from Latin.

Uni means "one." *Cornu* means "horn."

Xtreme Unicorn Sighting #5

Marco Polo's Unicorns Italian explorer Marco Polo traveled to China in the late 1200s. He wrote about incredible beasts he saw along the way. He believed he saw unicorns. He described them as big elephants with a horn. He said they lazed in mud. They kept their heads low like wild boars. Polo concluded these unicorns were ugly. They were nothing like the shining white unicorns of **folk tales**. The animals he described likely were rhinoceroses!

Typical unicorns have the body of a horse with a white coat. They may sport a spiraling horn, a goat's beard, a lion's tail, and cloven hooves.

Life as a Unicorn

The word "unicorn" appears in the Bible. Scholars translated the Hebrew word *re'em* as "unicorn." But the word could also mean "ox." Horse-like unicorns became widely used in Christian art during the **Middle Ages**. At that time, unicorns were symbols of purity.

Pliny the Elder was an ancient Roman author. In A.D. 77, he wrote about unicorns in his book *Natural History*. He described it as a fierce animal. It had "the body of a horse, the head of a stag, the feet of an elephant, the tail of a boar, and a single black horn three feet long in the middle of its forehead." He was probably describing a rhinoceros.

Over the centuries, stories emerged of unicorns that would rather die than be captured. In the 14th century, the unicorn became a symbol for Scotland's independence. By the 20th century, unicorns represented freedom of personal expression. Today, they are found on everything from notebooks and stickers to mugs and clothing.

writes about unicorns
A.D.
77

sees them on his travels
1290s

adopts unicorn as national animal
late
1300s

| Pliny the Elder | Marco Polo | Scotland |

late
1570s
acquires the Horn of Windsor

1741
no longer used in medicine

1981
to present
includes unicorns in franchise

Queen Elizabeth I   Alicorn powder   *My Little Pony*

LIFE AS A UNICORN FACT

The *My Little Pony* franchise combined unicorns and Pegasus to create horned, flying princess ponies. They are called alicorns.

Xtreme Unicorn
Sighting #4

Hunting the Unicorn In one European fairy tale, hunters try to catch a white unicorn. But it is too swift to be caught. So the hunters set a trap. They bring a young maiden into the forest. The unicorn is drawn to her. It puts its head in her lap. As she combs its mane, it falls asleep. The hunters catch it and take it to the king. But the unicorn escapes! It runs back to the forest.

XTRAORDINARY HISTORY

Unicorns have become popular in recent years. There are many books about brave unicorns. These mythical creatures often represent courage and self-confidence.

A group of unicorns is called a blessing.

UNICORN BLESSINGS

Unicorn Society

France's Lascaux grotto features many cave paintings. They are about 17,000 years old! Some people believe the art includes a unicorn. It is running with a group of aurochs, wild oxen that died out in 1627. The "unicorn" appears to have a single spiraling horn on its forehead. No one knows whether the drawing is a unicorn or an auroch.

The United Kingdom's **coat of arms** features a lion and a unicorn. The lion represents England. The unicorn represents Scotland. Long ago, England and Scotland fought. The lion became the symbol for England in the 1100s. The big cats are known for their strength. But unicorns are said to be able to defeat lions. So Scotland adopted the mythical creature as its national animal in the 1300s.

XEMPLARY SKILLS FACT

Unicorns are said to run faster than the speed of light.

The speed of light is 186,282 miles (299,792 km) per second!

XEMPLARY SKILLS

Unicorns are mysterious, magical, and beautiful. They have strong hearts. They run swiftly. They can become invisible. Unicorns are usually viewed as gentle. But some are fierce fighters.

Some legends say unicorns battled elephants and lions. Unicorns usually won these fights.

Unicorns have purple or blue eyes. If a person looked into a unicorn's eyes, he would not see his reflection. Instead, he would see the unicorn's forest home. Unicorns have keen hearing. A human cannot sneak into the forest undetected. The unicorn will always know.

At one time or another, most civilizations recognized unicorns as real animals. The Turkish *kartijan* was a ferocious unicorn. It was huge. The sound of its hooves was like thunder across the land. All animals feared the kartijan except the ringdove. This bird's song could put the kartijan to sleep.

TOP FIVE XTREME UNICORN SIGHTINGS

Xtreme Unicorn Sighting #3

Unicorns in Asia Parts of Asia are home to mythical creatures that are similar to unicorns. The *qilin* of China, *kirin* of Japan, and *kỳ lân* of Vietnam are scaled creatures. Many have a lion's mane and a single horn. The qilin is usually gentle. Seeing one brings good luck and peace. In Japan, the kirin is the most powerful of all mythical beasts. Both of these creatures are said to hunt criminals, piercing them in the heart with their horns.

Today, unicorn sightings are rare. Still, some people believe these mythical beasts are real. But scientists have not yet proven their existence.

Unicorn Legacy

There are many real animals that look like unicorns. The extremely rare saola lives along the border of Vietnam and Laos in Southeast Asia. Its name means "spindle horns." Nicknamed the "Asian unicorn," it was discovered in 1992. Its horns can grow 20 inches (50.8 cm) long. Other animals mistaken for unicorns are rhinoceroses, okapis, and Arabian oryx.

Horns sold as alicorns during the Middle Ages were most likely from antelopes, oxen, or narwhals. In the 1570s, Sir Martin Frobisher gave a unicorn horn to Queen Elizabeth I. In actuality, it was a narwhal tusk. Frobisher found it while exploring Canada. The queen valued the gift, and it became known as the "Horn of Windsor."

Historiae Animalium is a five-part book. It was published between 1551 and 1587. It describes all the animals its author believed lived on Earth—including unicorns.

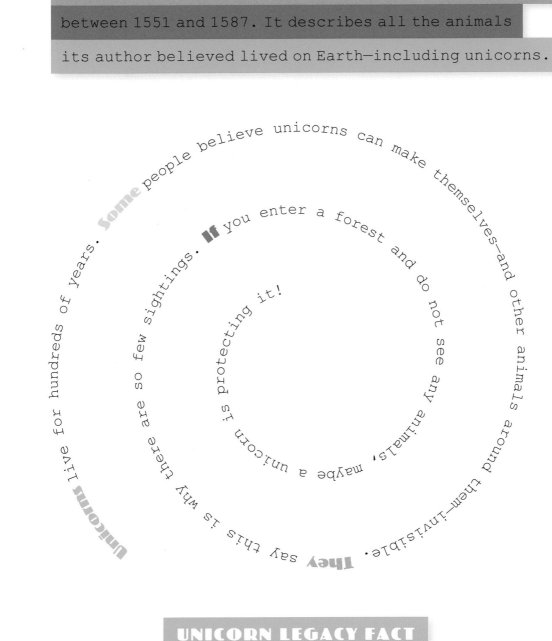

Some people believe unicorns can make themselves—and other animals around them—invisible. They say this is why there are so few sightings. If you enter a forest and do not see any animals, maybe a unicorn is protecting it! Unicorns live for hundreds of years.

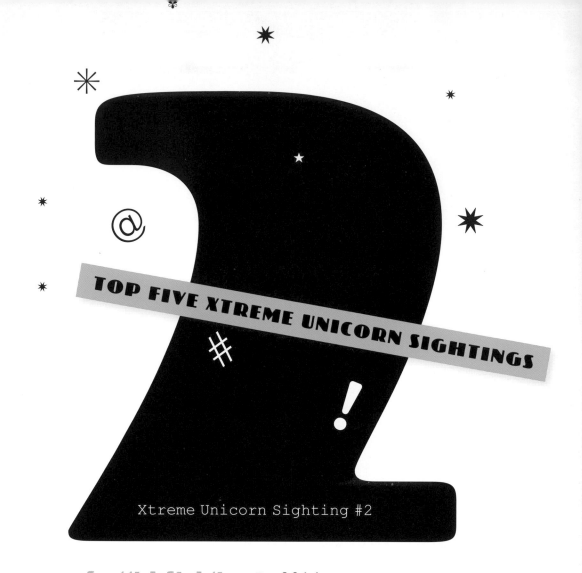

Xtreme Unicorn Sighting #2

Scottish Sighting In 2014, a man claimed he saw a unicorn near Wick in Caithness, Scotland. While hiking, the man briefly saw "a horse with a horn." The unicorn then trotted toward a lake south of the town. Tourists may be tempted to visit Wick to find the unicorn. But the man says they will be disappointed. He believes unicorns reveal themselves only to people who are not looking for them.

The 15th century "Unicorn Tapestries" hang on display at the Metropolitan Museum of Art.

The unicorn has long been associated with royalty in Scotland.

A unicorn questing license can be obtained from Michigan's Lake Superior State University.

Traditionally, unicorns are male.
Recently, some unicorns have been portrayed as female.

Unlike several other mythical creatures, unicorns do not harm people.

Legends say that if a person ever caught a unicorn, it would be impossible to tame.

Another mythical horse is Pegasus. He has wings but no horn.

No one has ever caught a unicorn, so scientists cannot study them.

Unicorns do not need to eat.
They get energy from the sun.

Voldemort, the villain in the Harry Potter series, drinks unicorn blood. He believes it will revive him—but it curses him.

Unicorns were featured on Scottish coins during the late 15th and early 16th centuries.

Built in the late 1600s, the throne of Denmark is said to feature unicorn horns.

Mongol leader Genghis Khan decided not to invade India after reportedly seeing a unicorn.

The eastern Hercules beetle is also called the unicorn

beetle. It is the largest beetle in the United States.

Xtreme Unicorn
Sighting #1

The Last Unicorn is a popular fantasy book. Written by Peter S. Beagle, it was published in 1968. It was made into a movie in 1982. In this story, a unicorn hears that a bull has captured all the other unicorns. She leaves her forest home to rescue them. Her journey is filled with danger. But she makes friends along the way. Together, they discover what happened to the other unicorns.

GLOSSARY

coat of arms – the official symbol of a family, state, nation, or other group

exotic – strange or unfamiliar

folk tales – timeless stories passed on by word of mouth

legends – traditional stories that are sometimes popularly considered history but are not proven to be factual

Middle Ages – a period in European history from c. 1100 to 1453

RESOURCES

Koranki, Susan. "The Mystical Unicorn of Scotland." http://www.scottish-at-heart.com/unicorn-of-scotland.html.

Lavers, Chris. *The Natural History of Unicorns*. New York: Harper Perennial, 2010.

Peabody, Erin. *Unicorns*. New York: Little Bee Books, 2018.

"Unicorns, West and East." American Museum of Natural History. https://www.amnh.org/exhibitions/mythic-creatures/land-creatures-of-the-earth/unicorns-west-and-east/.

INDEX

Long ago, unicorns were described as wild, angry beasts.